MAY YOU LIVE A LIFE YOU LOVE

COMPENDIUM
INCORPORATED

live inspired.

Written & Compiled by M.H. Clark

Designed by Sarah Forster

TAKE YOUR LIFE AND LIVE IT WELL

Be kind to yourself. Dream great dreams.
Listen to your heart. Celebrate your strengths.
Appreciate your talents. Delight in your own uniqueness.
Find time for joy. Give of yourself. Lean into the hard work.
Seize new opportunities. Find wonder.

MAY YOU LIVE A LIFE YOU LOVE.

MAY YOU CHERISH THIS LIFE WITH ALL YOUR HEAD AND ALL YOUR HEART

Life isn't about

finding yourself. Life is about creating yourself.

George Bernard Shaw

MAY YOU FIND WONDER

The only way to live is to accept each minute as an unrepeatable miracle, which is exactly what it is: a miracle and unrepeatable. Margaret Storm Jameson

SCATTERED EVERYWHERE

MAY YOU HAVE
HAPPY MEMORIES
THAT BRIGHTEN
EVERYTHING
THEY TOUCH

The memories I value most,
I don't ever see them fading.

Kazuo Ishiguro

The most important
things in life
aren't things.
Anthony J. D'Angelo

MAY YOU LEARN
TO RECOGNIZE ALL
THE DAZZLING AND
IMPORTANT THINGS

THAT YOUR EYES

CANNOT

SEE

MAY YOU BE SURROUNDED WITH PEOPLE WHO HELP YOU

GROW

I know there is strength
in the differences between us.
I know there is comfort
where we overlap.

Ani DiFranco

MAY YOU HAVE **IDEAS** SO **BIG** THAT THEY GROW

THEIR OWN WINGS

Don't be afraid of new ideas. Be afraid of old ideas. They keep you where you are and stop you from growing and moving forward. Concentrate on where you want to go, not on what you fear.

Anthony Robbins

You're alive...
That means you have infinite potential. Neil Gaiman

MAY YOU DELIGHT
IN SEEING
WHAT YOU ARE
CAPABLE OF

No matter what age you are, or what your circumstances might be, you are special, and you still have something unique to offer. Your life, because of who you are, has meaning.

Barbara de Angelis

GIFTS THAT ONLY YOU CAN GIVE

MAY YOU BE PROUD OF THE WORK YOU DO, THE PERSON YOU ARE, AND THE DIFFERENCE YOU MAKE

Don't look for miracles.
You yourself are the miracle.

Henry Miller

MAY YOU FIND WAYS TO
KEEP YOUR

AMS ALIVE AND WELL

Decide that you want it more than you are afraid of it.

Bill Cosby

MAY YOU LOVE YOURSELF DEEPLY FOR EVERYTHING YOU ARE

If we really love ourselves,
everything in our life works. Louise L. Hay

MAY YOU BE GENTLE
WITH OTHERS AND
GOOD TO YOURSELF

Be kind, for everyone you meet
is fighting a hard battle.

Ian MacLaren

The most beautiful people we have known are those who have known defeat, known suffering, known struggle, known loss, and have found their way out of the depths. These persons have an appreciation, a sensitivity, and an understanding of life that fills them with compassion, gentleness, and a deep loving concern. Beautiful people do not just happen.

Elisabeth Kübler-Ross

MAY YOU HEAL PAST HURTS AND EMBRACE NEW CHANCES

MAY YOU REALIZE THAT YOU ARE ANYTHING BUT

When there is no enemy within,
the enemies outside cannot hurt you.

African proverb

BREAKABLE

Knock the "t" off the "can't."

Samuel Johnson

MAY YOU
STARE
DOWN
YOUR
FEARS
TO UNDERSTAND
THEM AND
OVERCOME
THEM

MAY YOU TAKE EPIC

Security is not the meaning of life.
Great opportunities are worth the risk.

Shirley Hufstedler

CHANCES

MAY YOU GROW TO LOVE

THE CHALLENGES, TOO

Being on the tightrope is living; everything else is waiting.

Karl Wallenda

MAY YOU MASTER THE ART OF ACCEPTING SURPRISES AND LANDING GRACEFULLY

Nearly all the best things that came to me in life have been unexpected, unplanned by me. *Carl Sandburg*

Live with intention. Walk to the edge. Listen hard. Practice wellness. Play with abandon. Laugh. Choose with no regret. Appreciate your friends. Continue to learn. Do what you love. Live as if this is all there is. Mary Anne Radmacher

MAY YOU
ALWAYS
FIND
REASONS TO
LAUGH

MAY YOU LOVE

The world is round and the place which may seem like the end may also be the beginning.

Ivy Baker Priest

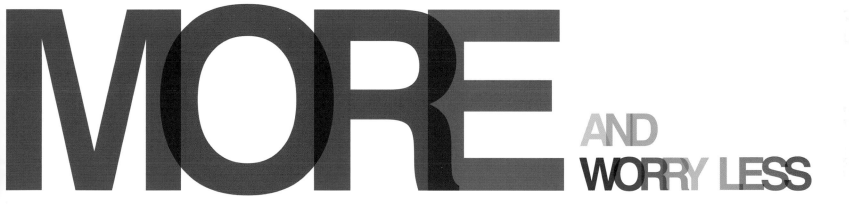

MORE AND WORRY LESS

MAY YOU HAVE THE
PATIENCE
AND THE
COURAGE
TO DO WHAT'S RIGHT

You have to do the right thing...
You may never know what results come from your action.
But if you do nothing, there will be no result.

Mahatma Gandhi

Life's challenges are not supposed
to paralyze you, they're supposed
to help you discover who you are.

Bernice Johnson Reagon

MAY YOUR DIFFICULTIES ONLY SERVE TO SHOW YOU WHAT'S WORTH FIGHTING FOR

MAY YOU
LEARN HOW TO
SHOW YOURSELF
DEEP KINDNESS

If your compassion does not include yourself, it is incomplete.

Jack Kornfield

AND UNCONDITIONAL LOVE

MAY YOU CULTIVATE

SILLINESS

I still listen to instinctual urges. I play with leaves.
I skip down the street and run against the wind.
I never water my garden without soaking myself.

Leo F. Buscaglia

MAY YOU BE SURROUNDED BY DELI

Ever since happiness heard

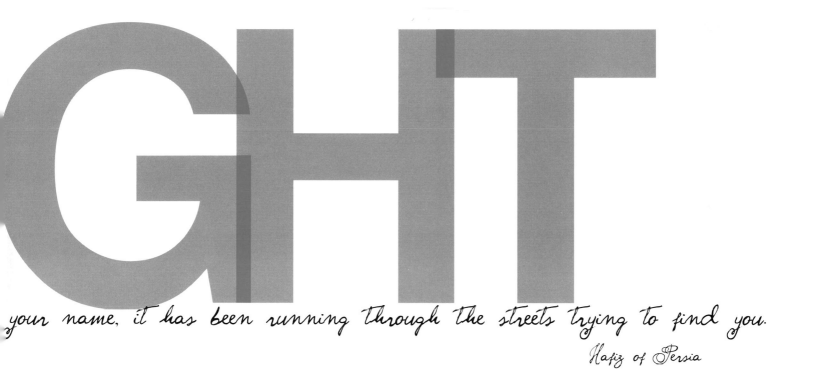

your name, it has been running through the streets trying to find you.

Hafiz of Persia

MAY YOU FIND A HOME FOR YOUR TALENTS IN THE WORLD

Don't live down to expectations.
Go out there and
do something remarkable.

Wendy Wasserstein

MAY YOU CULTIVATE DEEP GRATITUDE FOR ALL THE JOYS THE WORLD OFFERS

Gratitude can transform
common days into Thanksgivings,
turn routine jobs into joy,
and change ordinary opportunities
into blessings.

William Arthur Ward

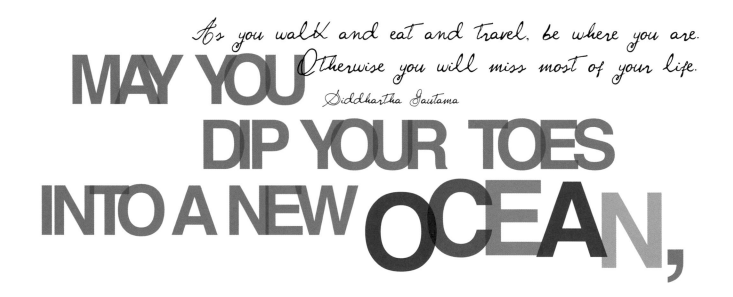

As you walk and eat and travel, be where you are.
Otherwise you will miss most of your life.
Siddhartha Gautama

MAY YOU
DIP YOUR TOES
INTO A NEW OCEAN,

DANCE UNDER A FOREIGN SKY, AND MARVEL AT THE WORLD

Be careful how you interpret the world: It is like that. Erich Heller

MAY YOU FIND THAT THE WORLD IS
SMALLER THAN YOU THOUGHT,
KINDER THAN YOU KNEW,
AND OFTEN ON YOUR SIDE

This is my life. It is my one time to be me

MAY YOU LIVE THE KIND OF LIFE YOU IMAGINE FOR YOURSELF

I want to experience every good thing. Maya Angelou

WITH SPECIAL THANKS TO THE ENTIRE COMPENDIUM FAMILY.

CREDITS:
Written by: M.H. Clark
Designed by: Sarah Forster
Edited by: Robin Lofstrom
Creative direction by: Julie Flahiff

ISBN: 978-1-935414-75-9

1st printing. Printed in China with soy and metallic inks.